FUNNY FILL-IN

MY PET ADVENTURE

NATIONAL GEOGRAPHIC

WASHINGTON, D.C.

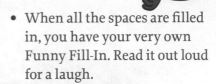

How to Play Funny Fill-In!

Love to create amazing stories? Good, because this one stars YOU. Get ready to laugh with all your friends—you can play with as many people as you want! Make sure to keep this book on your shelf. You'll want to read it again and again!

Are You Ready to Laugh?

- One person picks a story—you can start at the beginning, the middle, or the end of the book.

- Ask a friend to call out a word that the space asks for—noun, verb, or something else—and write it in the blank space. If there's more than one player, ask the next person to say a word. Extra points for creativity!

- When all the spaces are filled in, you have your very own Funny Fill-In. Read it out loud for a laugh.

- Want to play by yourself? Just fold over the page and use the cardboard insert at the back as a writing pad. Fill in the blank parts of speech list, and copy your answers into the story.

Make sure you check out the amazing **Fun Facts** that appear on every page!

Parts of Speech

To play the game, you'll need to know how to form sentences. This list with examples of the parts of speech and other terms will help you get started:

Noun: The name of a person, place, thing, or idea
Examples: tree, mouth, creature
*The **ocean** is full of colorful **fish**.*

Adjective: A word that describes a noun or pronoun
Examples: green, lazy, friendly
*My **silly** dog won't stop laughing!*

Verb: An action word. In the present tense, a verb often ends in –s or –ing. If the space asks for past tense, changing the vowel or adding a –d or –ed to the end usually will set the sentence in the past.
Examples: swim, hide, plays, running (present tense); biked, rode, jumped (past tense)
*The giraffe **skips** across the savanna.*
*The flower **opened** after the rain.*

Adverb: A word that describes a verb and usually ends in –ly
Examples: quickly, lazily, soundlessly
*Kelley **greedily** ate all the carrots.*

Plural: More than one
Examples: mice, telephones, wrenches
*Why are all the **doors** closing?*

Silly Word or Exclamation: A funny sound, a made-up word, a word you think is totally weird, or a noise someone or something might make
Examples: Ouch! No way! Foozleduzzle! Yikes!
*"**Darn!**" shouted Jim. "These cupcakes are sour!"*

Specific Words: There are many more ways to make your story hilarious. When asked for something like a number, animal, or body part, write in something you think is especially funny.

silly word

friend's name

celebrity's name

verb

noun

animal, plural

verb

insect, plural

something sticky

cartoon character

same friend's name

verb

noun

exclamation

CLUB PET RESORT

Welcome to Club Pet!

_____ vacation starts today—but not for _____ or me. Our
        silly word   *friend's name*

parents left us in charge of the family business, Club Pet Resort, a hotel for pets more pampered than

_____ . When my alarm buzzes, I run to _____ owners
        celebrity's name   *verb*

dropping off our pet guests. I have to dive under a(n) _____ to avoid a flock of
                                                              noun

_____ , then _____ to miss the _____ .
        animal, plural   *verb*   *insect, plural*

I collide into my friend, who is covered in _____—that's because (s)he likes to
                                                  something sticky

dress like _____ . All of sudden, _____ and I
              cartoon character   *same friend's name*

_____ face-first into a bale of hay for the horses. Yuck! We're covered in _____ .
        verb   *noun*

The parrot yells, "_____ !" and the place erupts in laughter. My friend and
                        exclamation

I take a bow. This is going to be one wild vacation.

- friend's name
- adjective
- animal, plural
- verb
- noun
- adverb ending in –ly
- verb ending in –s
- something wriggly
- body part
- electronic gadget
- something smelly
- noun, plural
- verb ending in –s
- something soft
- body part
- kind of game
- same electronic gadget
- large number

Kitchen Catastrophe

_____ and I know we'll rock our first task—dinnertime. The food looks _____ and
   friend's name   *adjective*

I'm ready to bring it out from the kitchen to our pet guests. Unfortunately, a flock of _____
                                                                                                              animal, plural

swoop in, causing the plates to _____ into the _____ . I _____ put
                                          verb   *noun*   *adverb ending in –ly*

them back in the right order, I think. But when a cat _____ a plate of _____ at
                                                              verb ending in –s   *something wriggly*

my _____ , I realize I mixed up the orders. The ferret gets a(n) _____ .
        body part   *electronic gadget*

We serve the hedgehog a bowl of _____ . The bunny scarfs down three of the snake's
                                          something smelly

_____ before it remembers it's a vegetarian. Suddenly the parrot _____ so hard
   noun, plural   *verb ending in –s*

a _____ shoots out its _____ . Before we can get all the pets the right meal, the dogs
     something soft   *body part*

start playing _____ with the tablecloth. Food flies everywhere. Fortunately, the ferret didn't
                  kind of game

eat the _____ so I use it to order a _____ -slice pizza for everyone.
           same electronic gadget   *large number*

- animal noise
- verb
- noun
- dog breed
- adverb ending in –ly
- noun
- noise
- another dog breed
- large vehicle
- type of dinosaur
- adverb ending in –ly
- body part, plural
- relative's name
- another body part
- large number
- celebrity's name
- your hometown

Fun Fact!

A DOG IN NOVA SCOTIA, CANADA, DISCOVERED **FOSSILIZED BONES** FROM A 300-MILLION-YEAR-OLD **REPTILE.**

Digging Dogs

The daily dog walk at Club Pet is always an adventure. Today is no exception. I throw the new _____ (animal noise)

toy for the dogs, who _____ (verb) after it, but they don't return. We find them digging behind a(n)

_____ (noun) . A(n) _____ (dog breed) digs so _____ (adverb ending in –ly) it buries me in _____ (noun) .

All of a sudden, we hear a(n) _____ (noise) and the earth gives way. We fall into a secret cavern. Then I

see a(n) _____ (another dog breed) holding a bone bigger than a(n) _____ (large vehicle) . It's a(n) _____ (type of dinosaur)

bone! We all jump into action and _____ (adverb ending in –ly) dig with our _____ (body part, plural) . Soon we uncover

a fossil older than _____ (relative's name) . I quickly post a picture on my _____ (another body part) -book page.

_____ (large number) people like the story. Soon, the reporters arrive along with _____ (celebrity's name) , who's

a paleontologist on the side. They take our picture to put in the _____ (your hometown)

Bulletin. We're famous!

friend's name

liquid

number

gymnastics move ending in –ing

verb

adjective

noun

year you were born

animal

vehicle

verb ending in –s

your height

your age

relative's name

something gross

adverb ending in –ly

NEPETALACTONE IS A CHEMICAL IN CATNIP THAT MAKES SOME CATS GO CRAZY FOR IT.

Kitty Pool

The new smoothie _____ and I created for the cats is a hit. It's made of _____ , fish, and
     friend's name   _liquid_

_____ teaspoon(s) of catnip. I think I might have accidentally added too much catnip to the last batch,
number

though, because now the cats are acting strange. They're _____ into the swimming
                   gymnastics move ending in –ing

pool! We try everything to _____ them out. We use a toy mouse, a ball of yarn, even a(n)
           verb

_____ _____ . Plus, they keep demanding more smoothies. After _____
 adjective   _noun_   _year you were born_

hours, we decide to bring in Trouble. He's a(n) _____ the size of a(n) _____ . He
               animal   _vehicle_

_____ into the pool and creates a(n) _____-tall tidal wave. _____ cats slosh
 verb ending in –s   _your height_   _your age_

out of the pool. Then Trouble falls asleep, snoring louder than _____ . The rest of the cats look
                    relative's name

at him as if he is _____ . They _____ scramble out of the pool and spend
     something gross   _adverb ending in –ly_

the rest of the day sunbathing instead. What a purr-fect afternoon!

- loud noise
  - kind of spice
- vehicle
  - type of plant
- something stinky
  - something gross
- verb
  - something slimy
- verb ending in –ing
  - dog breed
- feeling
  - kind of vegetable
- kind of meat
  - animal, plural
- body part
  - favorite cereal

Fun Fact! TO INCREASE THE BOND WITH THEIR DOG, SOME PEOPLE AND THEIR DOGS DO A STYLE OF YOGA CALLED DOGA.

Wacky Relaxation

_____ ! That's the unmistakable sound of Grandma _____ 's pet grooming _____ .
(loud noise) ....(kind of spice) ....(vehicle)

It runs on _____ -oil power, but smells like _____ power. Grandma arrives to lead
...............(type of plant) ....(something stinky)

the pets in a day of relaxation all dressed in tie-dye and smelling like _____ ! She definitely has
....(something gross)

a strange way of pampering pets at Club Pet. The pigs _____ when she throws them into a mud bath
....(verb)

that feels like _____ . Then the neighbor brings her yaks over for yoga class. Grandma puts me
.......................(something slimy)

to work _____ the chicken's nails. But when the _____ looks _____ about
............(verb ending in –ing) ....(dog breed) ....(feeling)

the _____ bath, Grandma shows me how to calm the pets with _____
.........(kind of vegetable) ....(kind of meat)

aromatherapy. By the end of the day, the animals look groovy. I dig the sheep's new dreadlocks and the far-out

beads on the _____ . But the peace signs on the cow's _____ blows my mind. As
.....................(animal, plural) ....(body part)

she drives away, Grandma yells, "Peace, love, and _____ ."
....(favorite cereal)

favorite snack food

friend's name

bird noise

animal noise

electronic gadget

silly word

large number

verb

car part

adjective

kind of fruit

something stinky

your name

your shoe size

celebrity's name

famous athlete

Fun Fact! SOME PARAKEETS CAN MIMIC WORDS AND WHISTLES. ONE PARAKEET COULD RECITE EIGHT NURSERY RHYMES.

Sidesplitter Twitter

"_____ !" That's what the parakeet calls _____ . Actually, it just said "_____ ," but
   favorite snack food   friend's name   bird noise

we just turned on the _____-o-Matic, a(n) _____ we ordered from _____
                        animal noise   electronic gadget   silly word

Magazine. It interprets what animals say. We're not really sure how it works because we didn't want to read

the _____-page instruction booklet. How hard can it be? We start secretly listening in on the noisy
    large number

birds. At first, they don't make a lot of sense. The birds say things like, "_____ _____
                                                         verb   car part

_____ ." Or my favorite, "Let's meet _____-face at the _____ farm on
   adjective   kind of fruit   something stinky

_____ Street for dinner." The device starts to beep so I smack it to get it to work better. All of a
   your name

sudden—*zap!* The parakeets' chatter turns into discussions about everything from finance to gardening tips.

As a joke, we post their comments online. Within _____ seconds, they're more famous than
                                            your shoe size

_____ ! Their parakeet podcast starts next week. I hear they're interviewing _____ !
   celebrity's name   famous athlete

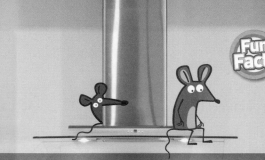

exclamation

   large number

adjective

   something stinky

kitchen appliance

   pop star

verb ending in –ing

   body part, plural

favorite drink

   adverb ending in –ly

verb ending in –ing

   electronic gadget

animal

   kind of rodent

your age

   adverb ending in –ly

A HAMSTER BLINKS ONE EYE AT A TIME.

Rodent Roundup

The door to the rodent cage is wide open—all the rodents have escaped! "_____ !" I cry and open
exclamation

a drawer to find a flashlight. But when I do, _____ pairs of _____ eyes are peering
large number adjective

out at me. That's when I notice the room smells like _____ . I look around and see the
something stinky

_____ is vibrating to the beat of _____ singing on the radio. Behind
kitchen appliance pop star

it, I discover a dozen guinea pigs _____ to the tunes. Just then a magazine with
verb ending in –ing

_____ poking out the bottom of it scurries past. I take a sip of my _____
body part, plural favorite drink

and _____ spit it out. The funky taste is from the hamster _____ in it.
adverb ending in –ly verb ending in –ing

I have to round up the rodents before things really get crazy. I grab a(n) _____ and tune in to
electronic gadget

the latest episode of _____ Idol. A _____ is in the top _____ . The rodents
animal kind of rodent your age

_____ gather around to watch. I settle in to watch with them. Successful roundup!
adverb ending in –ly

- reptile body part
  - adjective
- kind of snake
  - item of clothing
- verb ending in –s
  - something fancy
- verb
  - musical instrument
- your favorite song
  - verb ending in –ing
- friend's name
  - adjective
- verb
  - your favorite beverage
- kind of reptile, plural
  - body part
- item of clothing
  - silly word

Fun Fact! THE **RETICULATED PYTHON** CAN GROW TO BE ALMOST AS **LONG** AS A **SCHOOL BUS!**

Party Like a Python

We put on a lot of events at Club Pet. Tonight we're throwing a python party celebrating _____ (reptile body part) Day. We dress the snakes and lizards in their finest _____ (adjective) scales. I'm rocking my fake _____ (kind of snake) _____ (item of clothing). The chameleon _____ (verb ending in –s) everyone by dressing as a(n) _____ (something fancy). The snakes flick their tongues to the rhythm of the music. Soon everyone hits the dance floor. Pythons _____ (verb) and slither to the sound of the _____ (musical instrument) version of "_____ (your favorite song)." Fireflies add a special glow, _____ (verb ending in –ing) to the beat. _____ (friend's name) shows off some _____ (adjective) moves. If you haven't been to a python party, here's something to know. Never _____ (verb) the _____ (your favorite beverage). The _____ (kind of reptile, plural) swim in it! Just when we thought the party was over, everyone starts shedding their _____ (body part) or _____ (item of clothing). That's when the party becomes a _____ (silly word) fiesta. Everyone rocks the night away!

Zany Zoo Divas

Zelda the zookeeper wants her stars ready for their big television debut on _____'s

your hometown

Star Search. She brings them to Club Pet to prepare for the big day. Talk about divas! The lion refuses to touch

anything the color of _____'s hair. The monkey demands _____

celebrity's name _something soft_

carpeting. The giraffe refuses to perform until the _____ dances. While I chill the lion's

animal

_____ , Zelda prunes the ostrich's leafy lunch to look like _____'s

something sticky _famous person_

_____ . Suddenly, a(n) _____ erupts from the costume trailer.

body part _funny noise_

Startled, _____ wanders into the crocodiles' path carrying _____ cream

friend's name _favorite candy_

pies. They collide and the desserts fly into the air. Just as the pies _____ down, burying stars in

verb

a(n) _____ mess, the paparazzi arrive. Unfortunately, the stars' big debut winds up as a big

adjective

fashion "don't" in _____ Magazine.

pet's name

21

adjective

  kitchen utensil, plural

verb

  snack food

electronic gadget

  noise

kind of candy, plural

  adjective

body part

  adjective

garden tool

  verb ending in –s

something in your closet

  silly word

something wriggly

  noun

body part

  number

For movie night, all the pets are excited to watch the _____ mega hit *When* _____
                                                        adjective   kitchen utensil, plural

Attack. As the parrots _____ the _____, the goat turns on the
                              verb   snack food

_____ . A _____ fills the room when the lights go out and the movie starts.
electronic gadget   noise

Dogs crunch their _____ . The movie is so _____ that the rat's _____
                   kind of candy, plural   adjective   body part

never blinks. But the flick gets really _____ when a giant _____ _____
                                          adjective   garden tool   verb ending in –s

a(n) _____ . I reach into the snack bowl and scream, "_____ !" The
     something in your closet   silly word

lizards have replaced the popcorn with _____ ! We start the movie again. Just then, a
                                        something wriggly

giant ball of string rolls in front of the screen, and the cats rush to get it, but end up shredding the screen into

_____ . Fortunately, the horse has her back turned because she's too scared to watch. Turns out,
noun

her _____ makes an excellent screen! We give the movie _____ hooves up!
     body part   number

silly word

   color

verb ending in –s

   noun, plural

adverb ending in –ly

   noise

adjective

   something shiny, plural

body part

   favorite game

ocean animal, plural

   something sticky

verb ending in –s

   friend's name

adjective

   same something shiny, plural

Fun Fact! PEOPLE STARTED KEEPING **GOLDFISH** AS PETS IN CHINA OVER 2,000 YEARS AGO.

Sleeping With the Fishes

One minute I'm cleaning the aquarium's tiny treasure chest and the next thing I know, I've shrunk down and am sitting on top of it! Before I can yell "_____ (silly word)," a _____ (color)-tailed fish _____ (verb ending in –s) into me. I trip over a pile of _____ (noun, plural). All I see is teeth, so I _____ (adverb ending in –ly) back away! But the fish just nudges me, then plops down and says "_____ (noise)."

It is so _____ (adjective) to have a new friend. Inside the treasure chest, we find _____ (something shiny, plural). I put it on my _____ (body part). Then we play _____ (favorite game) with the _____ (ocean animal, plural). But I slip on snail _____ (something sticky) and hit my head. Suddenly, someone _____ (verb ending in –s) my face and shouts. Dogs, cats, and _____ (friend's name) surround me. Turns out I bumped my head cleaning the aquarium. *What a(n)* _____ (adjective) *dream*, I think, until I discover I'm still wearing _____ (same something shiny, plural) and the fish waves a fin at me!

- verb
  - large number
- year you were born
  - electronic gadget
- color
  - something squishy
- friend's name
  - adjective
- name of a country
  - food
- relative's name
  - your favorite toy, plural
- verb
  - verb ending in –ing
- favorite song
  - large number

Fun Fact! SOME **PARROTS** LIVE UP TO 80 YEARS.

Pulling Parrot Pranks

Mail time! I _____ (verb) open the phone bill and find it's _____ (large number) dollars. How could Club Pet have

used _____ (year you were born) minutes in one day? To find out, I set up a hidden _____ (electronic gadget) and

watch from another room. When the phone rings, a _____ (color) parrot answers, "Hello this is Club Pet.

We have your _____ (something squishy) ready" in a voice that sounds just like _____ (friend's name). Another

_____ (adjective) parrot pecks at the other phone. He's calling _____ (name of a country) long distance to order

_____ (food) for takeout! But before I can rush in and stop the pesky parrots, I hear a voice that sounds

like _____ (relative's name) over the loud speakers say, "Free _____ (your favorite toy, plural) for everyone!" All

the pets _____ (verb) into the room. As the parrots take turns _____ (verb ending in –ing) one another, I sneak

up behind them and unplug the phones. As punishment for all the trouble they've caused, I think I'll make

the parrots sing " _____ (favorite song) " _____ (large number) times.

silly word

something stinky

type of pet

noun

verb ending in –ing

room in a house

farm animal

adverb ending in –ly

body part

adjective

electronic gadget

piece of furniture

room in a house

household appliance

Fun Fact! LLAMAS ARE RELATIVES OF CAMELS. LIKE CAMELS, LLAMAS SPIT WHEN THEY ARE ANNOYED.

"_____ !" I shout when I sit in _____ on the couch. This is the second time. It

all started when I caught the _____ eating _____ and the hedgehogs _____

in the _____ . I yell, "Everybody go outside!" Soon the dogs are outside snoozing on the

_____'s backs, and the cat is draped across the hay. _____ , the farm

animals wander into the house. Now the llama is scratching its _____ against the furniture while

the _____ pony licks the _____ and a herd of cattle make themselves at home

on my _____ . And I have no idea what the pig is doing in the cat's _____ ,

but I'm not cleaning it up! I hope this ends soon. But after tonight I think everyone will be ready to switch

places again. Well, except for the goats. They're fascinated by the _____ .

relative's name

noun

heavy object

ocean animal

silly word

same relative's name

body part

verb

something that floats

adverb ending in –ly

adjective

something fast

famous athlete

your grade

ocean animal

flying animal

THE LONG-TAILED DUCK DIVES AS DEEP AS 200 FEET (60 M) TO FIND FOOD.

Duck Paddle!

_____ the duck hatched yesterday! And today this duckling is getting a swimming
　　relative's name

_____ . Problem is, its mother swims like a(n) _____ and she's afraid of water! So
　　noun　　　　　　　　　　　　　　　　　　　　　heavy object

Carl, the _____ from the local zoo, and I are teaching the duckling to swim. "_____,"
　　　　　ocean animal　　　　　　　　　　　　　　　　　　　　　　　　　　　　　silly word

Carl calls to _____ , who jumps right in. Carl holds the duckling up by its _____
　　　　　　same relative's name　　　　　　　　　　　　　　　　　　　　　　　　　body part

while I _____ a(n) _____ . The duckling _____ kicks, then sinks
　　　　verb　　　　　　something that floats　　　　　　　　　　adverb ending in –ly

again. This time, Carl dives in and demonstrates how to wiggle its _____ tail. It works! The duckling
　　　　　　　　　　　　　　　　　　　　　　　　　　　　　　　adjective

takes off faster than a(n) _____ and races through the water like _____ . Later
　　　　　　　　　something fast　　　　　　　　　　　　　　　　　　　　famous athlete

that day, she competes in the _____ annual water race—and wins! The judges compliment
　　　　　　　　　　　　　　your grade

the duckling for swimming like a(n) _____ . Tomorrow the duckling gets flying lessons with
　　　　　　　　　　　　　　　　ocean animal

the _____ !
　　flying animal

31

- favorite food, plural
- friend's name
- verb ending in –ing
- Australian animal, plural
- Arctic animal, plural
- animal noise
- African animal, plural
- adverb ending in –ly
- adjective
- direction
- verb ending in –s
- something hard
- silly word
- adverb ending in –ly
- vehicle
- planet
- number
- body part

Fun Fact! AN **AARDVARK'S TONGUE** CAN BE 12 INCHES (30.5 CM) LONG

CLUB Pet
it's a
Wild time
CaLL
555-1234

CLUB Pet
it's a
Wild time
CaLL
555-1234

"We're out of aardvark _____ (favorite food, plural) ," _____ (friend's name) announces. "We don't have aardvarks here,"

I say. My friend just points. There they are, _____ (verb ending in –ing) with the _____ (Australian animal, plural) . Then I

see _____ (Arctic animal, plural) scampering up the rock wall. A(n) _____ (animal noise) echoes across the field.

We turn to see a herd of charging _____ (African animal, plural) . They _____ (adverb ending in –ly) wave their

_____ (adjective) credit cards and gift shop souvenirs. Then a squirrel shimmies _____ (direction) on a

branch like a ninja. It _____ (verb ending in –s) a bag of _____ (something hard) then disappears into our resort.

That's when I realize my poster advertising "Club Pet—it's a wild time" worked. Although not as I intended.

All of a sudden, the aardvarks shriek, " _____ (silly word) !" pointing _____ (adverb ending in –ly) upward. A

_____ (vehicle) from _____ (planet) hovers _____ (number) inches above my _____ (body part) . That's

when I remembered I also tweeted, "@Club Pet it's out of this world!" Who knew they'd take my ad so literally?

- noun
  - animal
- adjective
  - verb
- kind of candy
  - verb
- adjective
  - body part
- verb ending in –s
  - verb ending in –ing
- verb ending in –s
  - verb ending in –s
- favorite color
  - item of clothing
- silly word

Fun Fact!

A TARANTULA LIQUEFIES ITS PREY AND THEN DRINKS IT LIKE A SMOOTHIE!

It's the middle of the night and the _____ alarm is blaring. A burglar! We stay safe upstairs while

noun

watching what happens on the _____-cam. The screaming alarm wakens the office insects.

animal

A swarm of _____ ants _____ in to save the day. Unfortunately, the burglar is

adjective _verb_

prepared. He tosses a handful of _____ at them and the ants _____ to it. Then

kind of candy _verb_

Fluffy the tarantula scampers up his leg and taps the _____ burglar on his _____.

adjective _body part_

The burglar _____ and pets Fluffy on the head. Luckily, the flock of _____ wasps

verb ending in –s _verb ending in –ing_

zoom to the rescue. They circle his head. He just laughs when one _____ into his ear.

verb ending in –s

Just when it appears as if nothing scares this guy, a breeze _____ the door open. In flutters

verb ending in –s

the most beautiful _____ moth. It lands on the burglar's _____. He cries

favorite color _item of clothing_

out, "_____" and races out the door.

silly word

type of sport

noise

small number

friend's name

food

body part

adverb ending in –ly

liquid

mythical creature

vegetable

same noise

noun

same liquid

dance move

Oinks on Ice

The pigs and I are preparing for our weekly water _____ lesson. Suddenly, we hear
(type of sport)

a _____ . Instantly, a bizarre cold snap causes the temperatures to plummet to _____
(noise) _(small number)_

degrees in seconds. Unfortunately, that's the exact moment _____ takes a lick
(friend's name)

of a(n) _____ . Now his/her _____ is frozen to it. Then I see a pig
(food) _(body part)_

_____ skate across the frozen _____ . Then another . . . and another!
(adverb ending in –ly) _(liquid)_

Watching the pigs skate with the grace of a(n) _____ , I become a little misty-eyed.
(mythical creature)

That's because I catch a whiff of them. Even frozen, they're still coated in the mashed _____
(vegetable)

from their lunch. Then I hear a _____ again. As fast as everything freezes, it unfreezes. The
(same noise)

sun bursts through the _____ and the ice shatters! The pigs sink into the _____ .
(noun) _(same liquid)_

Without missing a beat, the pigs start a water _____ .
(dance move)

- silly word
- friend's name
- large number
- favorite cartoon
- measurement of time, plural
- adjective
- verb ending in –ing
- temperature
- item of clothing
- noun
- silly word
- verb
- noun
- same friend's name
- relative's name
- adverb ending in –ly
- exclamation

Fun Fact!

IT IS ILLEGAL TO LET YOUR **DONKEY SLEEP** IN A **BATHTUB** IN **ARIZONA, U.S.A.**

Donkey Ride

Club Pet is holding its annual _____ Carnival. The main attraction is donkey gymnastics.
                                        silly word

_____ , the donkeys' coach, has the donkeys watch _____ hours of
friend's name   *large number*

" _____ " to get all their moves. I arrive _____ early so I
   favorite cartoon   *measurement of time, plural*

don't miss a thing. But just as I'm waiting for the competition to start, I see a(n) _____ balloon
                                                                                        adjective

_____ above me. Turns out the ferrets made a(n) _____ air balloon from my
verb ending in –ing   *temperature*

_____ . Because I am such a good _____ , the donkeys let me take the first
item of clothing   *noun*

ride. " _____ ," I say and _____ into the basket made from a broken _____ .
          silly word   *verb*   *noun*

_____ fills the balloon with hot air. Unfortunately, it smells like _____ 's
same friend's name   *relative's name*

feet. I shout _____ as I float higher and higher. Suddenly I drop through a crack in the
                adverb ending in –ly

basket. " _____ !" Fortunately, I land on the donkeys' gym mats. What a wild ride!
            exclamation

- snack food
  - silly word
- adjective
  - historical figure
- verb ending in –s
  - noun
- type of pet
  - body part
- friend's name
  - animal noise, plural
- pet treat
  - baby noise
- same snack food
  - exclamation
- adjective
  - verb ending in –ing
- something lightweight

Fun Fact!

ACCORDING TO **SUPERSTITION,** SHARING A BOWL OF MILK WITH **A FERRET** **CURES** WHOOPING COUGH.

40

Thanks to the ferret, a visit from _____ Jones, star of _____ TV's *Pet Psychic* show doesn't

snack food · silly word

go as planned. Because of his _____ wig, the psychic looks like _____ . Unfortunately,

adjective · historical figure

while the psychic prepares for the show, the ferret sneaks into the dressing room. He _____ the

verb ending in –s

psychic inside a(n) _____ , then snatches the psychic's wig and runs onstage with the microphone.

noun

Surprisingly, the camera and the crowd love him. The phony television star touches a _____'s

type of pet

_____ and _____ interprets the _____ saying, "You will win a giant

body part · friend's name · animal noise, plural

_____ !" The crowd yells, "Hip, hip, _____ !" and begs for more. Just as the ferret takes his

pet treat · baby noise

last bow, _____ Jones appears and yells, " _____ !" The crowd only laughs because

same snack food · exclamation

his _____ bald head sparkles like a crystal ball under the stage lights. The last time we see the

adjective

former star, he's _____ away faster than a _____ in a windstorm!

verb ending in –ing · something lightweight

THE WORLD'S LARGEST
PET RABBIT
WEIGHS 55 POUNDS (25 KG).

- cartoon character
  - kind of candy
- friend's name
  - animal
- number
  - adjective
- small number
  - verb
- type of plant
  - noun
- vegetable
  - verb
- noun
  - exclamation
- something slimy
  - verb
- verb

Bouncing Baby Bunnies

Bouncing baby bunnies might be as cute as _____ , but they're as squirmy as first graders
                                              cartoon character

after an all-you-can-eat _____ contest! So far _____ and I have played leap
                            kind of candy   friend's name

_____ and had a(n) _____-and-a-half legged race with them. I think teaching bunnies hopscotch
     animal   number

is the perfect solution to keep them _____ . It works for _____ seconds, but then the
                                          adjective   small number

bunnies _____ through the hotel and grab a roll of toilet paper made from _____ . They
            verb   type of plant

vault over every _____ and shrub at Club Pet, leaving behind a trail of paper. Chasing them around the
                     noun

_____ trees only causes them to _____ faster and unroll more paper. By now, toilet paper
   vegetable   verb

blankets the _____ . " _____ ," I sigh, and grab the hose. When I start blasting the paper, it
                 noun   exclamation

becomes as slick as _____ . The bunnies _____ through it playing a(n) _____
                      something slimy   verb   verb

-and-slide game. But soon the bunnies have played so hard they've tired themselves out and fall fast asleep!

- animal, plural
  - number
- adjective
  - noun
- verb ending in –ing
  - type of pet, plural
- adjective
  - animal
- noun
  - celebrity's name
- farm animal
  - your age
- another type of pet
  - number
- verb
  - noun, plural
- cartoon show
  - book title
- kitchen utensil, plural

TALENT SHOW

Fun Fact!

HEDGEHOGS
SPEND MOST OF THEIR LIVES
ON THE GROUND,
BUT THEY CAN ALSO SWIM
AND CLIMB TREES.

Pet Talent Show

After watching an episode of _____ *in Tiaras* on channel _____, we decide that
          animal, plural   number

Club Pet should put on a(n) _____ _____ show—minus the divas! The talent starts
                              adjective   noun

with the _____ _____. It's so _____ it'll be hard to
         verb ending in –ing   type of pet, plural   adjective

top. But Sparky the _____ gets a standing _____ for his impersonation of
                      animal   noun

_____. The _____ wows the judges in the formal wear competition with
 celebrity's name   farm animal

hot pink, _____-inch-tall high heels. Next, the _____ saunters onto stage. It's
           your age   another type of pet

wearing cowboy boots and a(n) _____-gallon hat. We almost _____ our _____
                               number   verb   noun, plural

when it tries to lasso a very angry cow. The mouse's dramatic reading from " _____ "
                                                                                cartoon show

brought the house down. For the finale, the hedgehogs belt out their version of _____
                                                                                    book title

while the horses play _____. What a great show!
                       kitchen utensil, plural

45

friend's name

adjective

kind of game

adverb ending in –ly

something gross

noun

piece of furniture

liquid

verb

type of pet, plural

same type of pet, plural

verb

liquid

same friend's name

something stinky

silly word

Fun Fact!

STUDIES SHOW THAT PEOPLE WHO HAVE PETS MAY LIVE LONGER THAN THOSE WHO DON'T.

Honey, I Shrunk the Horses

Our parents come home today. _____ (friend's name) and I want everything to be absolutely _____ (adjective),

but everything goes wrong. First, the Dalmatians start a game of _____ (kind of game). They

_____ (adverb ending in –ly) run through the organic spot remover I use to clean the _____ (something gross)

spills off the _____ (noun). That stuff really works. Unfortunately, the Dalmatians are now spot free,

too. Next the chameleons decide to blend in with the _____ (piece of furniture) so I can't find them. Before I can

think of what to do, the horses start a _____ (liquid) fight and accidently _____ (verb) the

_____ (type of pet, plural). The _____ (same type of pet, plural) _____ (verb) into the paint. Now we have

footprints everywhere. Just as my parents drive up, I turn on the hose and _____ (liquid) squirts out,

soaking my friend. Now _____ (same friend's name) smells like _____ (something stinky). Our parents hug us

and say, " _____ (silly word), it's just a typical day at Club Pet!"

Published by the National Geographic Society

John M. Fahey, *Chairman of the Board and Chief Executive Officer*
Declan Moore, *Executive Vice President; President, Publishing and Travel*
Melina Gerosa Bellows, *Publisher; Chief Creative Officer, Books, Kids, and Family*

Prepared by the Book Division

Hector Sierra, *Senior Vice President and General Manager*
Nancy Laties Feresten, *Senior Vice President, Kids Publishing and Media*
Jay Sumner, *Director of Photography, Kids Publishing*
Jennifer Emmett, *Vice President, Editorial Director, Kids Books*
Eva Absher-Schantz, *Design Director, Kids Publishing and Media*
R. Gary Colbert, *Production Director*
Jennifer A. Thornton, *Director of Managing Editorial*

Staff for This Book

Kate Olesin, *Project Editor*
James Hiscott, Jr., *Art Director*

Kelley Miller, *Senior Photo Editor*
Ruth Musgrave, *Writer*
Jim Paillot, *Illustrator*
Ariane Szu-Tu, *Editorial Assistant*
Callie Broaddus, *Design Production Assistant*
Margaret Leist, *Illustrations Assistant*
Grace Hill, *Associate Managing Editor*
Joan Gossett, *Production Editor*
Lewis R. Bassford, *Production Manager*
Susan Borke, *Legal and Business Affairs*

Production Services

Phillip L. Schlosser, *Senior Vice President*
Chris Brown, *Vice President, NG Book Manufacturing*
George Bounelis, *Senior Production Manager*
Nicole Elliott, *Director of Production*
Rachel Faulise, *Manager*
Robert L. Barr, *Manager*

Editorial, Design, and Production by Plan B Book Packagers

The National Geographic Society is one of the world's largest nonprofit scientific and educational organizations. Founded in 1888 to "increase and diffuse geographic knowledge," the Society's mission is to inspire people to care about the planet. It reaches more than 400 million people worldwide each month through its official journal, *National Geographic,* and other magazines; National Geographic Channel; television documentaries; music; radio; films; books; DVDs; maps; exhibitions; live events; school publishing programs; interactive media; and merchandise. National Geographic has funded more than 10,000 scientific research, conservation, and exploration projects and supports an education program promoting geographic literacy.

For more information, please call 1-800-NGS LINE (647-5463) or write to the following address:

National Geographic Society, 1145 17th Street N.W., Washington, D.C. 20036-4688 U.S.A.

Visit us online at www.nationalgeographic.com/books

For librarians and teachers: www.ngchildrensbooks.org

More for kids from National Geographic: kids.nationalgeographic.com

For information about special discounts for bulk purchases, please contact National Geographic Books Special Sales: ngspecsales@ngs.org

For rights or permissions inquiries, please contact National Geographic Books Subsidiary Rights: ngbookrights@ngs.org

ISBN: 978-1-4263-1683-8

Printed in Hong Kong

14/THK/1